Don't Skip Dessert:

Gluten-Free, Grain-Free, and Sugar-Free Sweet Treats

Don't Skip Dessert: Gluten-Free, Grain-Free, and Sugar-Free Sweet Treats

Copyright © 2012 Sherry Lipp

All rights reserved

Published by:

June Bug Publishing

Seattle, WA

ISBN: 978-1-300-23792-1

No portion of this book may be reproduced mechanically, electronically, or by any other means, without written permission of the publisher/author.

To order additional copies of this book please visit:

www.lulu.com

Table of Contents

Introduction	1
Kitchen Essentials	2 – 4
Baking with Almond Flour	4 – 5
Yogurt	5 – 6
Smoothies	**7 – 10**
Cakes & Cupcakes	**11 – 26**
Cookies & Bars	**27 – 39**
Candy	**40 – 44**
Pies & Tarts	**45 – 55**
Frozen Treats	**56 – 68**
Everything Else	**69 – 84**
Index	

Introduction

I have been following the Specific Carbohydrate Diet™ since October of 2000. Creating grain and sugar-free desserts has been a hobby. Desserts can be a particular challenge with the SCD Diet because sugar, wheat flour, baking powder, and milk are prohibited. Making desserts without these items was a new experience. It required a lot of trial and error to produce satisfying desserts.

This book shares some of my favorite SCD dessert recipes that I have refined over my years of being on the diet. Material for this cookbook is based on my website www.scdforlife.com

Please check with a physician before beginning a new diet program. This diet in no way replaces any medical care or treatment. Readers are encouraged to refer to *Breaking the Vicious Cycle* by Elaine Gottschall for detailed information on The Specific Carbohydrate Diet™.

Kitchen Essentials

Parchment Paper

Parchment paper is a baking lifesaver. The baked goods made with almond flour and honey tend to be sticky. Parchment paper makes cleaning up a breeze and prevents baked goods sticking to the pan.

Yogurt Maker

Yogurt is an essential part of the Specific Carbohydrate Diet. While it should be eaten regularly on its own, it also makes great desserts.

Ice Cream Maker

Using the 24-hour yogurt (see below) and an ice cream maker, you can create some great ice cream-like treats.

Baking Cups

Just like with parchment paper, these keep cupcakes and muffins from sticking to the pan.

Muffin Pan

I find that that making cupcakes and muffins is easier than making full-size cakes. Cupcakes cook more evenly than big cakes.

Cake Pans

Though cupcakes might be easier to cook, there are times when you are going to want to make a full-size cake. Keep two 8 or 9 inch round pans, one 9 x 13 inch cake pan, and one 8 x 8 inch cake pan on hand.

Cookie Sheets

Cookie sheets are perfect for cookies, biscotti, and scones.

Almond Flour

Almond flour is the easiest flour substitute for gluten and grain-free baking. It is not really "flour," but finely ground almonds. It's best to buy very fine almond flour.

Coconut Flour

Coconut flour is frequently used in gluten and grain-free baking. It is very light and works nicely for lighter desserts. Coconut flour absorbs more liquid and requires careful measuring of ingredients.

Honey

Honey is the only sweetener allowed on the SCD Diet. Buying in large quantities will help save money.

Baking Soda

Since baking power is not allowed, baking soda is used for cakes and cookies that need to rise a little.

Spices

Spices need to not have any added ingredients. For desserts it's good to have cinnamon, nutmeg, cloves, and ginger on hand.

Extracts

Vanilla and peppermint extract with no added sugar is essential for SCD baking.

Baking with Almond Flour

Baking with almond flour takes some getting used to, but it is not difficult.

The main thing to keep in mind is that baked goods will not have the same texture or flavor as their wheat flour counterparts.

Almond flour is heavier, contains natural oil, and creates a denser dessert. I have come to think of SCD desserts as something new, rather than expecting them to taste like wheat flour cakes and cookies.

Almond flour does not have a strong taste and will take on the desired flavor of your desserts.

The flour tends to burn a little more easily than regular flour. Ovens vary, so lowering the temperature or reducing cooking times will solve this problem.

Cookies and cakes baked with almond flour tend to "sweat" a little because of the natural oil in the almonds. This can be reduced by storing the baked goods in the refrigerator or freezer. The baked goods also can spoil if they are not refrigerated. I always refrigerate baked goods right away, and freeze them if they are not eaten within three or four days.

Baked goods made with almond flour are best if the almond flour is very fine. Different brands have different consistency, so it is good to experiment until you find one you like.

Yogurt

As outlined in *Breaking the Vicious Cycle,* yogurt is an important part of The Specific Carbohydrate Diet™. Commercial yogurt is not allowed on the diet. All yogurt eaten on SCD must be homemade, according to the directions outlined in the book (fermenting for 24 hours).

You can use any fat content milk, from skim to whipping cream, as a base for the homemade yogurt. I have only made yogurt with cow's milk, so all recipes in this book containing yogurt were made with cow's milk yogurt.

Different fat contents result in different textures and flavors of yogurt.

Skim milk yogurt is thin and the most sour in taste. I don't think it works as well for desserts, but it can certainly be used. The dessert may not be as creamy or sweet.

I use yogurt made from 2% milk most often. It has a nice thick texture and is creamy enough for most desserts, without having a lot of extra fat.

Yogurt made from whole milk makes a good frozen yogurt.

Yogurt made from one part whipping cream and one part half & half makes the most flavorful and creamy frozen yogurt. This frozen yogurt most resembles ice cream, in my opinion. Because of the high fat content I tend to save it for special occasions.

Yogurt made from 100% whipping cream is very thick and sweet. It also whips up a lot like regular whipping cream. It makes a great dessert topping.

In the cookbook you will sometimes see recipes calling for "dripped yogurt." This is a process of straining the yogurt through a cheese cloth or specialty yogurt strainer to get the liquid out. The longer the yogurt is strained, the thicker it will be.

Smoothies

Smoothies

Honey and Mint Tea Smoothie

Ingredients:

2 peppermint tea bags
1 ½ cups water
1 cup yogurt
1 tbsp honey

Preparation:

1. Boil water and add tea bag

2. Steep tea for 20 minutes

3. Pour tea into ice cube trays and freeze

4. Combine all ingredients in a blender until smooth

Peach Banana Smoothie

Ingredients:

1 cup frozen peaches
1 ripe banana
½ cup orange juice
½ cup yogurt

Preparation:

1. Combine all ingredients in blender

2. Blend until smooth

Tropical Smoothie

Ingredients:

½ cup frozen mango pieces
½ cup crushed pineapple
1 ripe banana
1 cup orange juice
½ cup yogurt
1 tbsp honey

Preparation:

1. Combine all ingredients in blender

2. Blend until smooth

Banana Ginger Smoothie

Ingredients:

1 ripe banana – frozen
½ tsp ginger
½ cup yogurt
½ cup orange juice

1 tbsp honey

Preparation:

1. Combine all ingredients in blender

2. Blend until smooth

Strawberry Banana Peanut Butter Smoothie

Ingredients:

1 banana – frozen
1 cup chopped strawberries
½ cup yogurt
2 tbsp peanut butter
1 tsp honey

Preparation:

1. Combine all ingredients in blender

2. Combine until smooth

Cakes & Cupcakes

Angel Food Cupcakes

Makes 10 Cupcakes

Ingredients:

12 egg whites (at room temperature)
2 tsp lemon juice
¼ tsp salt
½ cup honey
2 tsp vanilla
½ cup coconut flour

Preparation:

1. Preheat oven to 325°

2. Line a muffin pan with baking cups

3. Sift coconut flour twice in a small bowl. Set aside

4. Melt honey in a small saucepan until it is very thin

5. Beat the egg whites on high until foamy. Add vanilla, lemon juice, and salt. Beat until soft peaks form. The eggs whites should not be stiff. Slowly add the honey while continuing to beat on high. Beat for several minutes until stiff peaks form

6. Carefully fold in coconut flour

7. Pour batter into baking cups. Fill cups to the top

8. Bake for 30 – 35 minutes until cupcakes are golden brown on top

9. Cool on wire rack before removing from pan

10. Serve with fresh berries if desired

Apple Pudding Cake with Broiled Peanut Butter Frosting

Makes 8 inch square cake

Cake Ingredients:

¼ cup melted butter
1 large egg
½ cup honey
1 tsp cinnamon
¼ tsp ginger
¼ tsp cloves
¼ tsp salt
1 cup almond flour
½ tsp baking soda
½ tsp vanilla
2 cups chopped peeled apples
½ cup chopped walnuts

Cake Preparation:

1. Preheat oven to 350°

2. In a large bowl whip butter, egg, vanilla, and honey until frothy

3. In a separate bowl mix spices, almond flour, baking soda

4. Pour into wet ingredients and mix thoroughly

5. Stir in apples and walnuts

6. Bake for 45 – 50 minutes until toothpick inserted in middle of cake comes out clean

Broiled Topping Ingredients:

¼ cup melted butter
¼ cup honey
½ cup peanut butter (no sugar added)
2 tbsp plain yogurt
½ cup coarsely chopped walnuts
½ cup coconut flakes
½ tsp cinnamon

Preparation:

1. In a medium bowl – stir together all ingredients

2. Spread over warm cake

3. Place under broiler for 3 – 5 minutes until topping is just browned and slightly bubbly. Keep a close eye on it so it doesn't burn

4. Store cake in refrigerator

Jelly Cupcakes

Makes 9 - 10 cupcakes

Ingredients:

2 ½ cups almond flour
2 eggs
¼ cup butter - softened
½ cup honey
1 Tbsp pure vanilla extract
1 Tbsp lemon juice
½ tsp sea salt
½ tsp baking soda
½ cup SCD legal jam (page 83)

Preparation:

1. Preheat oven to 350°

2. Line cupcake pan with baking cups

3. Sift almond flour into a large bowl and stir in baking soda and salt

4. In a separate bowl mix eggs, butter, honey, vanilla, and lemon juice. Beat at medium speed for two minutes

5. Pour wet ingredients into almond flour mixture

6. Spoon batter into each baking cup so it is about $1/3$ full

7. Spoon a teaspoon of jam into the middle of each cupcake

8. Pour the remaining batter over the jam so each baking cup is $2/3$ to $3/4$ full

9. Bake for 30 – 35 minutes until tops are golden brown

Lime & Coconut Banana Cupcakes

Makes 12 cupcakes

Ingredients:

Cupcakes:

2 ½ cups almond flour
1 tsp baking soda
½ tsp salt
½ cup shredded coconut
½ cup butter – slightly softened
4 very ripe medium bananas
½ cup honey
1 tbsp vanilla
¼ cup yogurt
2 eggs
1 tsp apple cider vinegar
1 tsp lime juice

Topping:

¼ cup honey
1 tbsp lime juice
½ cup shredded coconut

Preparation:

1. Preheat oven to 350°

2. Line a muffin pan with baking cups and lightly grease the sides

3. Combine almond flour, salt, baking soda, and coconut in a large bowl

4. In a separate large bowl mash banana and add butter honey, vanilla, yogurt, eggs, vinegar, and lime juice.

5. Blend on medium speed for two minutes

6. Slowly add the almond flour mixture while beating on low speed

7. Blend for about a minute until everything is combined, but do not over mix

8. Pour batter into baking cups so they are $2/3$ full

9. Bake for 25 – 30 minutes or until toothpick inserted in the middle comes out clean

10. Cool on wire racks

11. While cupcakes cool, prepare topping

12. Combine all topping ingredients in a small bowl and allow to stand for 20 minutes

13. Spread a thin layer of the topping over the cupcakes

14. Place under broiler for 2 – 3 minutes, keeping a close eye on them because coconut can burn easily. Remove just when it turns slightly brown

15. Allow to cool for 20 minutes before removing from pan

Peanut Butter Surprise Cupcakes

Makes 10 – 12 cupcakes

Ingredients:

½ cup coconut flour
¼ tsp baking soda
½ tsp salt
4 eggs
½ cup honey
¼ cup butter softened
1 tbsp vanilla
Peanut Butter Bottom ingredients:
½ cup peanut butter
½ tsp vanilla
3 tbsp honey

Preparation:

1. Preheat oven to 350°

2. Line a muffin pan with ten baking cup liners

3. Mix dry ingredients in a small bowl

4. Beat the rest of the cake ingredients in a large mixing bowl until smooth. Slowly add the dry ingredients and beat at medium speed until creamy

5. In a small bowl, mix the Peanut Butter Bottom ingredients. Stir until well combined

6. Spoon a teaspoon of the peanut butter mixture into the bottom of the baking cups

7. Pour ¼ cup of the batter over the peanut butter mixture

8. Bake for 20–24 minutes until toothpick comes out with only a few crumbs. The tops of the cupcakes should also be dry and firm

Pumpkin Walnut Cupcakes

Makes 12 Cupcakes

Ingredients:

2 ½ cups almond flour
½ tsp baking soda
½ tsp salt
½ cinnamon
½ tsp nutmeg
¼ tsp cloves
¼ tsp ginger
3 eggs
1 tsp vanilla
½ cup honey
½ tsp lemon juice
1 cup fresh cooked pumpkin
½ cup chopped walnuts
Cinnamon for sprinkling on top

Preparation:

1. Preheat oven to 350°

2. Place pumpkin in a large bowl

3. Mash up pumpkin so it is soft

4. Add the rest of the ingredients, except walnuts, and beat with electric mixer for three or four

minutes. It's okay with this muffin recipe to blend well

5. Line a muffin pan with baking cups

6. Pour batter by ¼ cupfuls into the baking cups

7. Top muffin batter with chopped walnuts

8. Sprinkle with a little cinnamon

9. Bake for 18 – 23 minutes until toothpick inserted in the middle comes out clean

10. Cool in pan for 30 minutes before removing

Spice Loaf

Makes 1 loaf

Ingredients:

1 cup honey
½ cup coffee
½ cup butter
2 cups almond flour
½ tsp cinnamon
½ tsp cloves
½ tsp nutmeg
¼ tsp ginger
2 cups almond flour
1 ½ tsp baking soda
2 eggs - beaten
½ tsp vinegar

Preparation:

1. Preheat oven to 350°

2. Line the bottom of a loaf pan with parchment paper and lightly butter the sides

3. In a small saucepan combine honey, coffee, butter, and spices

4. Bring to boil and remove from heat

5. Cool until it is just slightly warm

6. In a large bowl combine almond flour, baking soda, eggs, and vinegar

7. Add liquid mixture to the almond flour and combine

8. Pour batter into loaf pan

9. Bake for 45 – 55 minutes or until toothpick inserted in the center comes out clean

10. Cool in pan for 15 minutes

11. Turn loaf out onto wire rack and cool completely before serving

Two-Layer Yellow Cake

Makes two 9 inch round layers

Ingredients:

2 ¼ cups almond flour
½ tsp salt
½ tsp baking soda
½ tsp lemon juice
¾ cup honey
2 eggs
1 tbsp vanilla
2 tbsp softened butter

Preparation:

1. Preheat oven to 350°

2. Line the bottom of two 9 inch round cake pans with parchment paper and lightly grease sides

3. Sift almond flour into a large bowl

4. Stir in salt and baking soda

5. In a separate bowl combine lemon juice, honey, eggs, vanilla, and butter

6. Beat until smooth

7. Stir the wet ingredients into the almond flour mixture

8. Stir until well combined

9. Pour batter in even amounts into the cake pans

10. Bake for 25 – 30 minutes until toothpick inserted in center comes out clean

11. Cool cakes in pans on wire racks until they are completely cooled

12. Carefully remove one layer onto a plate

13. "Frost." There are several choices here that are good substitutes for regular frosting. I personally like to use thickened yogurt with some fresh berries. You could also use yogurt whipped cream, peanut butter, or homemade SCD jam (no pectin)

14. Add second layer of cake on top of the filling

15. Top with more of your filling, fresh fruit, or yogurt whipped cream

Vanilla Berry Cake

Makes one 9 inch round cake

Ingredients:

½ cup coconut flour
¼ tsp baking soda
½ tsp salt
4 eggs
½ cup honey
⅓ cup softened butter
1 tbsp pure vanilla extract
1 cup mixed berries (strawberries, raspberries, blackberries, blueberries)

Preparation:

1. Preheat oven to 350°

2. Line bottom of 9 inch round cake pan with parchment paper

3. Mix dry ingredients in a small bowl

4. Combine eggs, honey, butter, and vanilla in a large bowl and blend with electric mixer on high speed for one minute

5. Stir in dry mixture and blend on medium speed for about 3 minutes

6. Stir in berries so they are distributed evenly throughout the batter

7. Pour batter into cake pan

8. Bake for 30 – 35 minutes until toothpick inserted in center of cake comes out clean

9. Cool cake in pan on wire rack for 45 minutes

10. If desired serve with whipped yogurt

Cookies & Bars

Cherry Vanilla Scones

Makes 12 – 15 Scones

Ingredients:

2 ½ cups almond flour
½ tsp baking soda
¼ tsp salt
¼ cup honey
1/3 cup melted butter
2 eggs
1 tbsp vanilla
½ cup chopped fresh red cherries

Preparation:

1. Preheat oven to 350°
2. Sift almond flour, baking soda, and salt into a large bowl
3. Add honey, butter, eggs, and vanilla into a medium bowl
4. Blend until smooth
5. Pour into almond flour mixture
6. Stir until well combine
7. Stir in cherries
8. Line baking sheet with parchment paper

9. Drop by large spoonfuls (about a ¼ cup) onto baking sheet about two inches apart

10. Bake for 13 – 17 minutes until toothpick inserted in center comes out clean

Lemon Blueberry Bars

Makes 12 bars

Ingredients:

Bottom Layer:

1 ½ cups almond flour
¼ tsp sea salt
2 tbsp melted butter
1 ½ tbsp honey
1 tbsp pure vanilla extract

Filling:

¼ cup honey
3 eggs
¼ cup melted butter
½ cup lemon juice
2 cups blueberries

Preparation:

1. Preheat oven to 350°

2. Lightly oil 8 x 8 inch glass baking dish

3. Combine all the ingredients for the bottom layer in a medium bowl

4. Stir well, until everything is combined

5. Press dough into the bottom of the baking dish so it makes an even layer

6. Bake for 15 minutes, until it is firm and slightly golden.

7. While bottom layer is baking, prepare filling

8. In a medium mixing bowl combine eggs, honey, melted butter, and lemon juice

9. Beat with electric mixer on high speed for 2 – 3 minutes until frothy

10. Pour mixture over baked bottom layer

11. Drop blueberries into mixture so they are spread out evenly over the dessert

12. Bake for 20 – 25 minutes until it is golden and appears set

13. Allow to cool for 30 minutes

14. Place in refrigerator for two hours until it is set

15. Store in refrigerator

Lemon Pecan Butter Cookies

Makes 20 - 25 Cookies

Ingredients:

½ cup honey
½ cup butter (softened but not melted)
2 eggs
1 tbsp fresh lemon juice
2 ¼ cups almond flour
1 tsp cinnamon
1 tsp baking soda
½ tsp salt
½ cup chopped pecans
a few pecan halves for garnish

Preparation:

1. Preheat oven to 350°

2. Cream together honey and butter – it should resemble frosting

3. Beat eggs and add to the honey-butter mixture

4. Add lemon juice, mix well

5. Add almond flour, cinnamon, baking soda, salt and chopped pecans, stir to combine

6. Line a baking sheet with parchment paper

7. Spoon dough by tablespoonfuls onto baking sheet about 2 inches apart

8. Place a pecan half on the top of each cookie

9. Bake for 12 – 14 minutes until cookies are browned on the bottom and slightly firm to the touch. Cookies will be soft, but shouldn't seem raw

10. Cool on wire rack

Nut Squares

Makes 10 – 12 bars

Ingredients:

2 cups whole mixed nuts (walnuts, filberts, pecans, almonds, cashews)
1 tbsp vanilla
$2/3$ cup honey
½ cup butter – room temperature
1 tsp cinnamon

Preparation:

1. Preheat oven to 375°

2. Coarsely chop nuts

3. Place butter, honey, and vanilla in a bowl

4. Beat with electric mixer for one or two minutes until butter is whipped

5. Mix butter mixture with nuts and cinnamon

6. Stir until well combined

7. Spread mixture evenly in an 8 or 9 inch baking dish

8. Bake for 12 – 15 minutes until golden brown

Nutty No-Bake Cookies

Makes 15 – 20 cookies

Ingredients:

¼ cup butter
1 cup peanut butter (no sugar added)
$^2/_3$ cup honey
1 cup almond flour
½ cup sliced almonds
½ cup chopped walnuts
½ up chopped pecans
1 tsp vanilla extract

Preparation:

1. Melt butter, peanut butter, and honey over medium heat in a medium saucepan

2. Stir in almond flour and nuts

3. Mix well and remove from heat

4. Stir in vanilla

5. Use tbsp to scoop 1 inch mounds onto parchment paper lined baking sheet.

6. Allow cookies to cool to room temperature

7. Place cookies in refrigerator for at least 2 hours until they are firm

8. Store cookies in refrigerator

Peppermint Biscotti with Frosting

Makes about 2 dozen biscotti

Biscotti Ingredients:

3 cups almond flour
1 tsp baking soda
¼ tsp salt
¼ cup melted butter
½ cup honey
2 eggs
1 tsp peppermint extract

Preparation:

1. Preheat oven to 350°

2. Line a baking sheet with parchment paper

3. Combine almond flour, baking soda, and salt in a large bowl

4. In a separate bowl combine melted butter, honey, eggs, and peppermint extract

5. Pour into almond flour mixture

6. Stir until well combined

7. Form dough into two flat wide loaves about an inch high on the baking sheet

8. Bake for 25 – 30 minutes until loaves are golden brown

9. All to cool completely – about 45 minutes to an hour

10. Slice the loaves at an angle to make biscotti

11. Place biscotti back on the baking sheet so it is lying on one side

12. Bake for 10 – 15 minutes, turn and bake for another 10 – 15 minutes. Biscotti should be crisp, but they will harden a little more as they cool

13. Remove from oven and cool completely before frosting

Peppermint Frosting Ingredients:

½ cup coconut butter
2 tbsp honey
1 tbsp butter
½ tsp peppermint extract

Preparation:

1. Combine coconut butter, honey, butter, and peppermint extract in a small saucepan

2. Stir over medium heat until coconut butter and regular butter are melted

3. Stir constantly and don't let the mixture get too hot or it will turn brown

4. It will only take 3 – 5 minutes for everything to melt

5. Remove from heat

6. Spread over biscotti

7. Place in refrigerator until frosting is hardened

8. Store biscotti in refrigerator

Spiced Cashew Blondie Bites

Makes 25 – 30 Bites

Ingredients:

1 cup cashew butter (make sure it is SCD safe - no sugar!)
1 egg
1 very ripe medium banana - chopped
¼ cup honey
½ tsp vanilla
½ tsp baking soda
⅛ tsp salt
½ tsp cinnamon
¼ tsp cloves
¼ tsp nutmeg
⅛ tsp ginger

Preparation:

1. Preheat oven to 350°

2. Line a mini-muffin pan with mini-baking cups (you will have to do a few batches, you can use two pans at a time if you have them)

3. Combine all ingredients in a large bowl

4. Blend on low speed for several minutes until all ingredients are well blended bananas are incorporated throughout

5. Drop by teaspoonfuls into baking cups so they are just over half full

6. Bake for 12 – 15 minutes until bites feel firm on top

7. Remove from pan and allow to cool

8. If you don't have a mini-muffin pan you can use a regular size muffin pan and increase baking time to 25 – 30 minutes

Strawberry Jam Bars

Makes 12 bars

Ingredients:

1 cup honey
½ cup butter softened
2 eggs
½ tsp vanilla
2 ¼ cups almond flour
1 tsp cinnamon
1 tsp baking soda
¼ tsp salt
¾ cup chopped walnuts
1 cup SCD legal jam (page 83)

Preparation:

1. Cream together butter and honey

2. Add eggs and vanilla

3. Beat for one minute

4. In a separate bowl add flour, cinnamon, baking soda, and salt

5. Combine dry ingredients with wet ingredients

6. Stir until well combined or use flat paddle of stand mixer

7. Stir in walnuts

8. Refrigerate dough for 30 minutes

9. Preheat oven to 350°

10. Spread cold dough into 8 inch square baking dish

11. Use a knife to swirl jam around the top of the dough

12. Bake for 20 – 25 minutes until it is golden and firm on top, toothpick inserted in center should be clean

13. Cool on wire racks for 30 minutes before cutting into squares

Candy

Coconut Butter Candy

These candies are a great substitution for chocolate, and just as satisfying!

Makes 10 – 15 candies depending on size

Ingredients:

½ cup coconut butter
2 tbsp honey
½ tsp vanilla extract
1 tbsp butter

Preparation:

1. Combine all ingredients in a small saucepan

2. Stir constantly over medium heat until coconut butter and regular butter are melted

3. Stir until well combined. This only takes about five minutes

4. Line a mini-muffin pan with mini-baking cups

5. Pour mixture into baking cups

6. Freeze for several hours

7. Store candy in freezer or refrigerator (allow to thaw a little before eating if storing in freezer)

Peanut Butter Cups

Ingredients:

Coconut Butter Candy mixture
SCD Peanut Butter (pure ground peanuts – no added sugar)

Preparation:

1. Prepare candy as above

2. Spoon ½ tsp peanut butter into bottom of baking cups

3. Pour coconut candy mixture over peanut butter

4. Freeze for several hours

5. Store candy in freezer or refrigerator

Nut Clusters

Ingredients:

Coconut Butter Candy
Raw mixed nuts (almonds, filberts, macadamia nuts, pecans walnuts etc.)

Preparation:

1. Prepare coconut candy as above

2. Line regular size muffin pan with baking cups

3. Fill bottom of baking cups with nuts

4. Pour candy mixture over nuts

5. Freeze for several hours

6. Store candy in freezer or refrigerator

Peppermint Cups

Ingredients:

Coconut Butter Candy (omitting vanilla extract)
Pure Peppermint Extract (no added sugar)

Preparation:

1. Prepare candy as above, omitting vanilla and adding peppermint extract

2. Line mini-muffin pan with mini-baking cups

3. Pour candy mixture into baking cups

4. Freeze for several hours

5. Store candy in freezer or refrigerator

Peanut Butter Fudge

Makes 12 – 16 pieces

Ingredients:

1 cup peanut butter
¼ cup butter
¼ cup coconut butter
¼ cup honey
¼ cup yogurt
1 tbsp vanilla

Preparation:

1. Add butter and peanut butter to a medium saucepan

2. Stir over medium heat until melted

3. Stir in honey and yogurt

4. Stir until yogurt is dissolved and mixture begins to darken and thicken, 4 – 5 minutes

5. Remove from heat

6. Stir in vanilla

7. Pour into a 8 x 8 inch baking dish

8. Refrigerate for several hours until set

9. Cut into pieces

10. Store in refrigerator

Pies & Tarts

Cherry Cashew Cheesecake

Makes 9 inch cheesecake

Ingredients:

Crust:

1 cup whole almonds
2 tsp vanilla
1/3 cup honey
¼ cup butter – room temperature

Filling:

1 ½ cups cashews
¼ cup lemon juice
1/3 cup coconut oil
1 tsp vanilla
1/3 cup honey

Topping:

2 cups cherries – pitted (frozen cherries will also work)
¼ cup honey
¼ tsp lemon juice
½ tsp cinnamon
¼ tsp vanilla

Preparation:

1. Soak cashews in 6 cups of water overnight

2. Preheat oven to 375°

3. Coarsely chop almonds

4. Place butter, honey, and vanilla in a bowl

5. Beat with electric mixer for one or two minutes until butter is whipped

6. Mix butter mixture with almonds

7. Spread mixture evenly over the bottom of a 9" cake pan

8. Bake for 10 – 12 minutes until golden brown, set aside

9. In a medium saucepan melt the coconut oil with the honey over low heat

10. Place the melted coconut butter, soaked cashews, lemon juice, and vanilla in a blender

11. Puree mixture until very smooth – this will take several minutes

12. Pour mixture over crust

13. Freeze overnight

14. Remove mixture from freezer 30 minutes before serving

15. Place all topping ingredients in a saucepan

16. Cook over medium heat until cherries are soft and bubbly, stir constantly

17. Remove from heat

18. Allow to cool before serving on top of the cheesecake

Date Nut Torte

Makes 9 inch Torte

Ingredients:

2 cups nuts (pecan, hazelnut, walnut, or macadamia)
12 - 14 Medjool dates (chopped and pitted)
1/3 cup water
½ cup honey
1 tsp vanilla
2 tsp lemon juice
1 tsp cinnamon
¼ tsp salt
3 eggs

Preparation:

1. Preheat oven to 400°

2. Spread nuts out in even layer on baking sheet

3. Roast nuts for 5 – 7 minutes until they are lightly browned

4. Increase oven temperature to 425°

5. Lightly oil a 9 inch pie pan

6. Add dates and water to a small saucepan

7. Heat over medium heat for 5 – 7 minutes until dates are very soft

8. Remove from heat

9. Stir in honey, vanilla, lemon juice, vanilla, cinnamon, and salt

10. Lightly beat eggs

11. Stir into date mixture and combine well

12. Stir in nuts

13. Pour into pie pan

14. Bake for 10 minutes

15. Reduce heat to 325°

16. Bake for another 20 – 25 minutes until torte is set in the middle

Easy Apple-Pear Pie

Makes 3 – 4 servings

Ingredients:

2 medium baking apples (Honeycrisp, Braeburn, Jonagold)
1 medium pear (Anjou, Bosc)
¼ cup chopped walnuts
½ cup almond flour
½ tsp cinnamon
¼ tsp nutmeg
½ cup strained yogurt
½ tbsp lemon juice
¼ cup honey

Preparation:

1. Preheat oven to 350°

2. Peel apples and pears and slice thin

3. Combine apples, pears, walnuts, and almond flour in a large bowl with the cinnamon and nutmeg

4. In a separate bowl combine yogurt, lemon juice, and honey

5. Beat for a minute on medium speed with an electric mixer

6. Fold yogurt mixture into the fruit mixture

7. Pour mixture into an 8 inch pie pan or a medium casserole dish and spread into an even layer

8. Sprinkle a little more cinnamon on top

9. Bake for 30 – 40 minutes until fruit is tender and top is golden

Lime Tart

Makes 8 servings

Ingredients:

¾ cup almond flour
3 eggs
¾ cup honey
¾ cup fresh lime juice
4 tbsp melted butter

Preparation:

1. Preheat oven to 350°

2. Place all ingredients in a large bowl

3. Mix with electric mixer at high speed for a couple minutes

4. Pour into an 8 inch pie pan

5. Bake for 30 – 35 minutes until pie is set and slightly golden

6. Allow to cool before serving

7. Store in refrigerator

Live Berry Pie

Makes 9" Pie

Ingredients:

Crust:

1 ¼ cups chopped Medjool dates
1 ½ cups almond flour
2 tbsp shredded coconut
1 tsp cinnamon

Pie:

¼ cup chopped Medjool Dates
4 – 5 medium very ripe bananas
½ tsp lemon juice
2 tbsp almond butter
2 tbsp coconut flour
1 ½ cups berries (chopped strawberries, raspberries, blueberries)

Preparation:

Crust:

1. Place dates, almond flour, and coconut into food processor. Process until everything sticks together (you can also use a stand mixer with the flat beater blade)

2. Press mixture into 9" glass pie pan. Press evenly across the bottom of the pan and up the sides. Should be about a quarter inch thick (or a little thicker on the bottom)

3. Place the pie pan in the refrigerator while you prepare the filling

Filling:

1. Mash bananas with the lemon juice

2. Place dates, mashed bananas, almond butter, coconut flour, and ½ cup of the berries in a food processor (or stand mixer bowl – use flat blade), and process until just smooth

3. Pour mixture into chilled pie crust

4. Spread rest of berries over mixture

5. Place in refrigerate for at least 2 hours before serving

6. Store in refrigerator

**Variation: Use one kind of berry, or add other fruit such as mangoes.

Poached Pear and Brie Dessert Pizza

Makes 2 servings

Ingredients:

Crust:

½ cup almond flour
1 egg
1 tsp honey
¼ tsp cinnamon

Topping:

1 pear (Anjou, Bosc)
½ cup orange juice
½ cup water
2 tbsp honey
½ tsp cinnamon
¼ tsp cloves
¼ tsp ginger
6 slices brie
¼ cup chopped walnuts

Preparation:

1. Preheat oven to 350°

2. Combine almond flour, egg, honey, and cinnamon in a medium bowl

3. Line a baking sheet with parchment paper

4. Spoon mixture onto parchment paper

5. Place another piece of parchment paper on top of the mixture and press down to spread dough into a 7 – 8 inch circle about a ¼ inch thick

6. If the dough is too sticky to peel the top paper off, it can be left on while the crust bakes

7. Bake for 7 – 8 minutes until crust is solid and slightly browned

8. Remove from oven and peel off parchment paper

9. Allow to cool while preparing the topping

10. Peel pear and slice thin

11. In a small saucepan combine orange juice, water, spices, and one tbsp of the honey

12. Drop pear slices into the liquid and simmer over medium-low heat for about 10 minutes, until pear is soft but not falling apart

13. Remove from heat, remove the pear slices from the saucepan

14. Spread the remaining honey over the baked crust

15. Place brie slices over the honey around the pizza

16. Place the pear slices over the pizza

17. Spread the chopped walnuts evenly over the pizza

18. Sprinkle with cinnamon

19. Bake for 15 minutes

Frozen Treats

Frozen Yogurt

Frozen yogurt is simple to make. You basically mix yogurt with honey, and add your desired flavors. I like to drip the yogurt for 6 – 14 hours before making the frozen yogurt mixture. This takes some of the liquid out and gives it a creamier texture.

You can use any yogurt you like from non-fat to whipping cream and half & half (I wouldn't use pure whipping cream yogurt because it has too much air in it and the texture is not quite right frozen). The more fat in the yogurt, the more of an ice cream-like texture it will have.

Basic Vanilla Frozen Yogurt

Makes about 2 pints

Ingredients:

4 cups dripped yogurt
¾ cup of honey (use ½ cup if you like a tarter flavor)
1 tbsp pure vanilla extract

Preparation:

1. Place ingredients in blender and mix until smooth.

2. Pour into ice cream freeze and process according to manufacturer's directions.

Peppermint Frozen Yogurt

Ingredients:

4 cups dripped yogurt

¾ cup honey
1 tsp peppermint extract

Preparation:

1. Combine all ingredients in blender and mix until smooth.

2. Pour into ice cream freezer and process according to manufacturer's instructions.

Strawberry Frozen Yogurt

Ingredients:

2 ½ - 3 cups dripped yogurt
4 cups whole strawberries (makes 2 cups pureed)
¼ cup orange juice
½ cup honey
1 tbsp pure vanilla extract

Preparation:

1. Place strawberries in blender and puree

2. Pour strawberries through strainer to get rid of the seeds

3. Add strawberries back to blender

4. Add the rest of the ingredients

5. Blend until smooth

6. Pour into ice cream freezer and process according to manufacturer's directions

The Best Banana Frozen Yogurt

This recipe takes a little bit of work, but it is well worth the effort!

Makes about 2 pints

Ingredients:

6 cups yogurt (made with half & half and whipping cream)
3 medium-large bananas
¾ cup honey
1 tbsp vanilla

Preparation:

1. Strain yogurt for 24 hours before making frozen yogurt mixture. Yogurt will be very thick – almost like cream cheese

2. Place whole unpeeled bananas in freezer the night before making yogurt

3. Take bananas out of freezer several hours before making frozen yogurt mixture. They should be completely thawed. Freezing and thawing the bananas brings out the flavor of the bananas

4. Once the bananas and yogurt are ready place them in the bowl of a stand mixer. If you don't have a stand mixer you can use a regular electric mixer

5. Add the honey and vanilla

6. Whip on high speed for 3 – 4 minutes until the yogurt fluffs up just a little

7. Pour mixture into ice cream freezer and make according to manufacturer's directions

Banana Bon Bons

Makes 12

Ingredients:

1 cup very thick yogurt (preferably strained overnight)
2 very ripe medium bananas
3 tbsp honey
1 tsp vanilla
Sliced almonds for topping

Preparation:

1. Place all ingredients except almonds in a large bowl

2. Beat on high speed for 3 – 4 minutes until creamy and smooth

3. Line mini-muffin pan with mini-baking cups

4. Spoon yogurt mixture into cups so they are filled to the top

5. Top yogurt with sliced almonds

6. Freeze in pan for several hours

7. Once the bites are solid you can transfer them to a closed container

Bananas Foster Sundae

For assembly you will need:

For each serving

2 Sweet Vanilla Biscuits (recipe follows)
"Bananas Foster" (recipe follows)
½ cup Vanilla Frozen Yogurt (pages 57 - 59)
Cashew butter (Peanut Butter or Almond Butter may be substituted)

Sweet Vanilla Biscuits Ingredients:

Makes 12 – 15 biscuits depending on how big you make them.

2 ½ cups almond flour
½ tsp salt
½ tsp baking soda
¼ cup honey
¼ cup melted butter
2 eggs
1 tsp pure vanilla extract

Preparation:

1. Combine almond flour, salt, and baking soda in a large bowl

2. In a smaller bowl, combine honey, melted butter, eggs, and vanilla

3. Whisk until well mixed

4. Pour wet ingredients into bowl with almond flour mixture

5. Stir until all ingredients are thoroughly combined.

6. Place bowl in refrigerator and chill for 30 minutes to one hour

7. Preheat oven to 350°

8. Line baking sheet with parchment paper

9. Scoop dough by large tablespoonfuls and roll into a ball with your hands

10. Place a couple inches apart on baking sheet

11. Bake for 15 – 20 minutes until tops are golden and firm to the touch. Toothpick inserted in the middle should come out clean

Bananas Foster Ingredients:

For each serving

1 ripe banana
1 tbsp butter
1 tsp honey
½ tsp cinnamon

Preparation:

1. Melt butter in a small saucepan over medium heat.

2. Slice bananas into the melted butter.

3. Add honey and cinnamon.

4. Stir constantly until bananas are soft and butter and honey forms a thick sauce.

5. Remove from heat.

Preparation of Sundae:

1. Slice two sweet biscuits and place face up on a plate

2. Spread a little cashew butter on the biscuits

3. Pour warm bananas over biscuits, reserving a little for the top of the yogurt

4. Top bananas with frozen yogurt.

5. Spoon the remaining bananas over the yogurt

Fried "Ice Cream"

Makes Two Servings

Ingredients:

1 cup frozen yogurt (pages 57 – 59)
1 egg
½ cup chopped walnuts
½ cup chopped pecans
¼ cup shredded coconut
Vegetable oil for frying

Preparation:

1. Allow frozen yogurt to soften a little (10 – 15 out of freezer)

2. Form yogurt into 4 golf ball-sized balls

3. Wrap in plastic wrap, place in a container, and place in freezer

4. Freeze for several hours or overnight

5. After freezing yogurt – beat egg in a small bowl

6. Mix nuts and coconut in a medium bowl

7. Take yogurt out of freezer and roll each ball in the egg and then roll it in the nut/coconut mixture

8. Place balls back in container and freeze again for several hours or overnight

9. When you are ready to fry the yogurt – heat ½ - 1 cup of vegetable oil in a small saucepan

10. Once the oil is hot use a slotted spoon to carefully put one ball at a time in oil. It only takes about 5 seconds to fry it. Turn the ball over so it is fried on both sides. This goes very quickly so be careful not to let it burn – the nuts can burn very quickly

11. Drain on paper towel briefly, then place back in freezer

12. Repeat with the other 3

13. Store in freezer until ready to serve

14. Serve with fresh fruit if desired

Frozen Banana Ice Cream Sandwiches

Makes one sandwich

Ingredients:

1 ripe banana
½ cup homemade frozen yogurt of your choice (pages 57 – 59)

Preparation:

1. Peel banana and slice in half

2. Place one half of banana on parchment paper on flat surface

3. Place another sheet of parchment paper on top of banana

4. Use the bottom of a large pan or pot to carefully press down on banana to flatten it out

5. Don't press too hard or banana will break. The banana should be fairly thick – ¼ - ½ inch

6. Repeat with other half of banana

7. Carefully place bananas in freezer (leaving them on the parchment paper is easiest) and freeze for 30 minutes to one hour

8. About 20 – 30 minutes before assembling sandwiches, remove yogurt from freezer so it can soften. You don't want it to melt, you just want it soft enough to be spreadable

9. Remove bananas from freezer

10. Spread yogurt on one half of banana and then top with the other half

11. Press down gently

12. Place sandwich back in freezer for a couple of hours until yogurt is firm and bananas are completely frozen

Frozen Strawberry Banana Pie

Makes 9 inch pie

Ingredients:

Crust:

2 cups almond flour
¼ tsp salt
3 tbsp melted butter
1 egg – beaten
1 tsp vanilla
2 tbsp honey

Filling:

1 ¼ cups chopped strawberries
1 medium ripe banana

2 tbsp orange juice
¼ cup honey
½ tsp vanilla
1 ½ cups strained yogurt

Preparation:

1. Preheat oven to 350°

2. Combine all crust ingredients in a large bowl

3. Form dough into a ball

4. Press dough into a 9' pie pan, evenly covering the bottom and sides

5. Bake for 10 minutes until crust is firm and golden

6. Puree 1 cup of the strawberries and the banana in a blender

7. Add the orange juice, honey, yogurt, and vanilla

8. Blend until smooth

9. Pour into baked crust

10. Fold in remaining chopped strawberries

11. Cover with foil and freeze for at least 3 hours until pie is firm

12. To serve, remove pie from freezer and allow to stand at room temperature for 10 minutes to soften

13. To store pie in freezer wrap in another layer of foil or place in freezer bag

Orange Yogurt Freeze

Makes one serving

Ingredients:

2 cups yogurt
2 – 4 tbsp honey (to taste)
4 – 6 tbsp orange juice
1 tsp vanilla
Fresh fruit and nuts for topping

Preparation:

1. Strain yogurt for at least 3 hours so it is very thick and creamy

2. Stir in honey, orange juice, and vanilla

3. Place in freezer for 2 to 3 hours – stir half way through freezing

4. Remove from freezer 10 minutes before serving

5. Top with fresh fruit and nuts

Everything Else

Baked Apples

Makes 4 servings

Ingredients:
4 large baking apples (Honeycrisp, Braeburn, Jonagold)
1 tsp cinnamon
¼ tsp nutmeg
¼ tsp ginger
¼ tsp cloves
¼ cup honey
½ tsp lemon juice
¼ cup chopped walnuts or pecans
¼ cup peanut or almond butter
¼ cup raisins
1 ½ tbsp butter
1 cup apple cider

Preparation:

1. Preheat oven to 325°

2. Mix spices, honey, lemon juice, chopped nuts, nut butter, and raisins in a small bowl to make filling

3. Core apples, making sure not to pierce the bottom

4. Remove skin one half inch around the top of the apple by the opening

5. Fill each of the apples with an equal amount of the filling

6. Divide butter into 4 pieces and place on top of the filling of each apple

7. Place apples in a square baking dish

8. Pour apple cider around the apples

9. Cover apples with foil

10. Bake for 45 – 60 minutes until apples are tender

11. Allow to cool slightly before serving

Baked Yogurt

Makes 1 ½ cups

Ingredients:

1 cup dripped yogurt – very thick
¼ cup chopped dates
2 tbsp raisins
¼ cup chopped walnuts, almonds and/or pecans
1 tbsp honey
2 tbsp orange juice

Preparation:

1. Preheat oven to 350°

2. Combine all ingredients

3. Spread into a 5" round baking dish (or use custard cups)

4. Bake for 30 minutes

5. Allow to cool for 30 minutes

6. Pour off any accumulated liquid

7. Chill in refrigerator until firm

8. Serve as is or use as spread for sliced apples

Crepes with Berry Filling

Crepes Ingredients:

Makes 7 – 8 Crepes

¼ cup plus two tbsp of almond flour
5 eggs
2 tbsp water
1 tsp vanilla
1 tbsp honey
$1/8$ tsp salt
½ tsp cinnamon
butter for frying

Preparation:
1. Place all ingredients in a large mixing bowl. Beat on medium speed until they are well mixed

2. Place batter in refrigerator for 15 - 30 minutes. Stir batter again before cooking

3. Heat an 8 inch pan over medium heat. Melt about one tsp of butter in the pan

4. Spoon two tablespoons of batter into the pan and tilt the pan to spread the batter in a thin layer over the pan

5. Cook for 45 seconds to one minute until batter is set

6. Carefully flip crepe and cook the other side for 10 - 15 seconds. It will take some practice to flip the crepes. If they fold over while flipping you can carefully unfold them

7. When crepe is done carefully slide it onto a plate. Melt more butter in the pan before cooking each crepe

8. Place a piece of parchment paper between each crepe to stack them. If you are not going to use the crepes right away you can roll them in the parchment paper, place them in a sealed bag or container and store them in the refrigerator (maybe just until the next day, I wouldn't store them for long)

Berry Filling Ingredients:

Makes 1 cup

¾ cup blueberries
1 cup sliced strawberries
1 tbsp honey
2 tsp lemon juice
¼ cup apple cider

Preparation:

1. Place all ingredients into a small sauce pan

2. Bring to a boil. Boil rapidly for 4 - 5 minutes until liquid is reduced to a thick sauce. Allow to cool

3. Place a spoonful of sauce in middle of the crepe

4. Fold both sides over, and flip the crepe over so flaps are on the bottom

5. Top with a little more sauce

6. Optional: top with plain yogurt and fresh berries for garnish

Lemon Curd

Makes 4 – 6 servings

Ingredients:

3 eggs
¼ cup honey
6 tbsp butter – room temperature and cubed
½ cup lemon juice

Preparation:

1. Place eggs and honey in a large bowl

2. Beat on high speed for 7 – 8 minutes until eggs are pale yellow and thick

3. Pour into medium saucepan

4. Add butter and lemon juice

5. Cook over medium heat

6. Stir constantly until butter is melted and mixture thickens

7. Just as it starts to bubble remove from heat (don't let it boil)

8. Pour into large bowl or individual serving dishes

9. Refrigerate for several hours until curd is set

Peach Crisp

Makes 6 – 8 servings

Ingredients:

Filling:

2 lbs sliced peaches – fresh or frozen
½ cup honey
1 tsp cinnamon
½ tsp lemon juice
1 tbsp coconut flour

Topping:

1 cup almond flour
½ cup chopped pecans
1 tsp cinnamon

½ cup cold butter - diced
⅛ tsp salt

Preparation:

1. Preheat oven to 350°

2. In a large bowl, combine peaches, honey, cinnamon, lemon juice, and coconut flour

3. Stir well

4. Pour mixture into a large baking dish

5. In a medium bowl combine all the topping ingredients. Because we are using honey, the topping will not be as crumbly as a traditional crisp

6. Spread topping over peach mixture

7. Bake for 60 – 70 minutes until topping is set and peaches are bubbly

8. Serve warm or allow to cool completely

Pumpkin Custard

Makes 4 servings

Ingredients:

1 ½ cups cooked pumpkin
1 cup dry curd cottage cheese
4 eggs
1 tsp vanilla
¼ cup honey
½ tsp cinnamon
¼ tsp cloves
¼ tsp ground ginger
¼ tsp nutmeg
Extra cinnamon and nutmeg for top of custard

Preparation:

1. Preheat oven to 350°

2. Combine all ingredients in blender and blend until smooth. I like to blend the dry curd with the eggs first to get it as smooth as possible

3. Pour mixture into four custard cups

4. Sprinkle a little cinnamon and nutmeg on top

5. Place custard cups in a large baking dish

6. Fill baking dish with water until it comes half way up the cups

7. Bake for 35 minutes then increase heat to 375°

8. Bake for 10 – 15 more minutes until custard is set

9. Allow to cool before serving

Shortcake Stuffed Baked Peaches

Makes 4 – 6 servings

Ingredients:

3 or 4 large peaches (depends on how large you can find)
2 ½ cups almond flour
½ tsp baking soda
¼ cup melted butter
¼ cup honey
2 eggs
1 tsp vanilla
A little extra honey
Cinnamon
Butter

Preparation:

1. Preheat oven to 375°

2. Combine almond flour, salt, and baking soda in a large bowl

3. Add melted butter, vanilla, and honey

4. Whisk eggs and pour into bowl

5. Mix well

6. Slice peaches in half. Remove pits. Scrape out the area that surrounded the pit

7. Place peaches in a glass baking dish. For easy cleanup line the baking dish with foil or parchment paper

8. Drizzle a little honey over the peaches and sprinkle with cinnamon

9. Scoop batter on top of the peaches so it fills the hollow of the peach and covers the top in a thick layer

10. Sprinkle a little more cinnamon over the batter

11. Bake for 30 minutes, until shortcake is golden brown on top

12. Reduce heat to 350°

13. Add a little (like ¼ - ½ tsp) butter to the tops of the shortcakes. Cover dish with aluminum foil and bake for an additional 10 minutes

Allow cooling a little before serving, but it is good served warm.

Spiced Applesauce

Makes about 2 cups

Ingredients:

4 apples (Granny Smith, Fuji, Golden Delicious or mixture of all)
½ cup apple cider
1 tsp cinnamon
¼ tsp cloves
¼ tsp ginger
¼ tsp nutmeg
1 tbsp lemon juice

Preparation:

1. Peel and chop apples
2. Combine with lemon juice in slow cooker
3. Add apple cider and spices
4. Stir to combine
5. Cook on high setting for 2 – 3 hours until apples have formed a thick sauce (or cook on low for 3 – 5 hours)
6. Stir and pour into a bowl
7. Allow to cool before serving

Strawberry Shortcake

Ingredients:

Shortcake – *Makes 12 cakes*

2 ½ cups almond flour
½ tsp salt
½ tsp baking soda
½ tsp cinnamon
¼ tsp ginger
¼ cup butter (softened)
¼ cup honey
1 tsp lemon juice
2 eggs

The amount of the rest of the ingredients will depend on how many shortcakes you are making.

You will need:

Sliced strawberries
Lemon juice
Yogurt made from whipping cream (or yogurt made from part whipping cream, part half & half)
Honey

Preparation:

Shortcake:

1. Preheat oven to 350°

2. Line muffin pan with baking cups

3. Stir almond flour, salt, baking soda, and spices in a large bowl

4. Mix butter, honey, lemon juice, and eggs in a medium bowl

5. Whisk until well mixed

6. Stir wet ingredients into the dry and stir until combined

7. Pour batter into baking cups so they are about ½ to ⅔ full

8. Bake for 20 - 25 minutes until toothpick inserted in center comes out clean

9. Cool before assembling shortcakes

10. Slice strawberries - about a cup of sliced strawberries per person

11. Place strawberries in a bowl and stir with a little lemon juice - about a ¼ tsp per cup of strawberries

12. Allow to sit while you prepare the whipping cream

13. Beat whipping cream yogurt with a little honey to taste. Beat until it is light and fluffy. It will come out pretty light, especially if you are using yogurt made with 100% whipping cream. Use about a ½ cup (before whipping) per person with about a ½ tsp of honey each

14. Cut shortcake in half

15. Place one half on a plate or in a bowl. Top with sliced strawberries and a spoonful of the whipped yogurt

16. Add another layer of strawberries and yogurt

17. Top with other half of shortcake. Add a little more whipped yogurt and a couple of strawberries for garnish

No Pectin Strawberry Jam

Makes about 3 cups

Ingredients:

4 cups whole strawberries
1 medium apple
¼ cup water
½ - ¾ cup honey
2 tsp lemon juice

Preparation:

1. Place Strawberries and water in large pot

2. Peel and cut up apple into very small pieces

3. Add apple to strawberries

4. Cook over medium heat until strawberries and apples break down and start to bubble - stirring constantly

5. Reduce heat to medium low

6. Add honey and lemon juice

7. Simmer for 30 - 60 minutes to reduce liquid - stir occasionally

8. If desired, use an immersion blend to blend berries for a few seconds

9. Remove from heat

10. Pour into freezer jars

11. Allow to cool for at least 30 minutes before placing in freezer or refrigerator

12. Freeze or refrigerate for several hours or overnight before serving

13. If freezing - allow to thaw for a couple hours before serving

Index

Angel Food Cupcakes 12
Apples
- Apple Pudding Cake 13
- Baked Apples 70
- Easy Apple-Pear Pie 50
- Spiced Applesauce 80

Baked Yogurt 71
Bananas
- Banana Bon Bons 60
- Banana Ginger Smoothie 9
- Bananas Foster Sundae 61
- Frozen Banana Ice Cream Sandwiches 65
- Frozen Strawberry Banana Pie 66
- Lime & Coconut Banana Cupcakes 17
- Peach Banana Smoothie 8
- Strawberry Banana Peanut Butter Smoothie 10
- The Best Banana Frozen Yogurt 59

Basic Vanilla Frozen Yogurt 60
Cakes
- Apple Pudding Cake 13
- Spice Loaf 21
- Two-Layer Yellow Cake 23
- Vanilla Berry Cake 25

Candy
- Coconut Butter Candy 41
- Nut Clusters 42
- Peanut Butter Cups 42
- Peanut Butter Fudge 44
- Peppermint Cups 43

Cherry Cashew Cheesecake 46
Cherry Vanilla Scones 28
Coconut Butter Candy 41'
Cookies & Bars
- Cherry Vanilla Scones 28
- Lemon Blueberry Bars 29
- Lemon Pecan Butter Cookies 31
- Nut Squares 32
- Nutty No-Bake Cookies 33
- Peppermint Biscotti 34
- Spiced Cashew Blondie Bites 37
- Strawberry Jam Bars 38

Crepes with Berry Filling 72
Cupcakes
- Angel Food 12
- Jelly 15
- Lime & Coconut Banana 17
- Peanut Butter Surprise 19
- Pumpkin Walnut 20

Date Nut Torte 48
Easy Apple-Pear Pie 50
Fried "Ice Cream" 63
Frozen Banana Ice Cream Sandwiches 65
Frozen Strawberry Banana Pies 66
Honey Mint Tea Smoothie 8
Jelly Cupcakes 15
Lemon
- Lemon Blueberry Bars 29
- Lemon Curd 74
- Lemon Pecan Butter Cookies 31

Lime & Coconut Banana Cupcakes 17
Lime Tart 51
Live Berry Pie 52
No Pectin Strawberry Jam 83
Nut Clusters 42
Nut Squares 32
Nutty No-Bake Cookies 33
Orange Yogurt Freeze 68

Peaches
- Peach Banana Smoothie 8
- Peach Crisp 75
- Shortcake Stuffed Baked Peaches 78

Peanut Butter
- Broiled Peanut Butter Frosting 13
- Peanut Butter Cups 42
- Peanut Butter Fudge 44
- Peanut Butter Surprise Cupcakes 19
- Strawberry Banana Peanut Butter Smoothie 10

Peppermint Biscotti 34
Peppermint Cups 43
Peppermint Frozen Yogurt 57

Pies & Tarts
- Easy Apple-Pear Pie 50
- Frozen Strawberry Banana Pie 66
- Lime Tart 51`
- Live Berry Pie 52
- Poached Pear and Brie Dessert Pizza 53

Pumpkin Custard 77
Pumpkin Walnut Cupcakes 20
Shortcake Stuffed Baked Peaches 78
Spice Loaf 21
Spiced Applesauce 80
Spiced Cashew Blondie Bites 37

Strawberries
- Frozen Strawberry Banana Pie 66
- Strawberry Banana Peanut Butter Smoothie 10
- Strawberry Frozen Yogurt 58
- Strawberry Jam 83
- Strawberry Jam Bars 38
- Strawberry Shortcake 81

Sweet Vanilla Biscuits 61
Tropical Smoothie 9
Two-Layer Yellow Cake 23
Vanilla Berry Cake 25

Yogurt
- Baked Yogurt 71
- Banana Frozen Yogurt 59
- Making Yogurt 5
- Orange Yogurt Freeze 68
- Peppermint Frozen Yogurt 57
- Strawberry Frozen Yogurt 58
- Vanilla Frozen Yogurt 57
- Yogurt and Ice Cream Makers 2